Diamonds in the Rough

By
Joe Kirchmyer

Printed in the United States of America

First Edition

Cover Design by Scott Webb

Edited by Patrick Klinck

Published by No Frills Buffalo
Nofrillsbuffalo.com

ISBN:
978-0578082240

This book is dedicated to all the coaches who have made a positive impact on the life of a child. Your actions have changed two lives — theirs and yours.

Foreword

What is wrong with youth sports these days? Why do participants and spectators alike pay so much attention to the win/loss column and championships? Somewhere along the way it seems the true value of youth sports — building strong positive character traits in the young men and women who participate — has been forgotten.

Dive into the anecdotal stories of Joe Kirchmyer's youth sports experiences in his book *Diamonds in the Rough* and you will find that the true value has not been lost on him and those he was privileged to coach. You will reach back in your own past and rekindle experiences that you had, and it will bring a smile to your face.

I enjoyed every scraped knee, every heartbreaking loss, and yes, some thrilling victories. But most importantly, I enjoyed hearing of young men and women who played the game because they had fun doing it. And along the way, they learned some lessons that helped them succeed beyond the field. I hope you find the same enjoyment as I.
Mark Kelso

(Mark Kelso played safety for the National Football League's Buffalo Bills from 1986-1993, appearing in four consecutive Super Bowls. He is currently color commentator for the Buffalo Bills radio network, director of advancement at St. Mary's High School in Lancaster, N.Y., and assistant coach for the school's varsity football team.

Introduction

Make no mistake about it, I love sports.

My lifetime of sporting memories dates back to when I was just five years old and joined my first baseball and bowling leagues. Having two older brothers (and later, a younger one) and a neighborhood full of kids helped me to develop my athletic skills rather quickly. We grew up in a modest Western New York neighborhood bordered by fields. One year, all of the neighbors got together and cleared a portion of the overgrown field behind our homes to make a playable baseball diamond, football field and even a hockey pond for the neighborhood kids and families to enjoy. It was a scene straight out of a Norman Rockwell painting, one that was repeated for many, many years.

I enjoyed our homemade facilities nearly every day, having only to jump the chain-link fence in our back yard to get to them.

If I recall correctly, I've participated in not only countless baseball and bowling leagues, but football, basketball, tennis, racquetball, broomball, soccer, softball, volleyball, floor hockey and roller hockey as well. And then there were the individual sports like judo, swimming and even gymnastics. Fishing was also a favorite pastime from a very early age and still is today.

I've played, I've coached and I've watched. And I've remembered. And now, I've gone deep inside my mind to bring you the best of nearly 50 years of memories. I hope you enjoy reading this compilation of humorous and sometimes uplifting short stories half as much as I've enjoyed living them and writing about them.

This book is dedicated to my wife, Maureen, who supports all of my crazy ideas whatever they may be, like writing a book. Actually, Maureen always says I could have written *Marley & Me*. I guess I could still do that, but it would be called *Rudy & Me* ... and I'd be sued. You'll read more about the adventures of Rudy, our beloved Golden Retriever, later.

And to my son, Andrew, and daughter Lauren. Until you have kids of your own, you'll have no idea how proud

I am of both of you. Continue to aim high and be the amazing people that you are. And to my brothers, Bill, Mark and Jeff, who share my love for sports and, for some unknown reason, the New York Mets (some sort of birth defect, I suspect). And to my parents, Bill and Lucy, who raised four crazy little boys and somehow turned us into pretty good men. My dad died far too young at the age of 54, but I'll always remember him for never saying no to a game of catch in the yard or a hike through the fields behind our house. To this day Mom is always there for us, no matter what we need.

To my friends mentioned throughout this book ... I hope you take everything in the good humor that it was intended. If not, write your own book! Special thanks to my good friends Scott Webb who illustrated the cover, and Pat Klinck for his editing work.

And finally, to my former colleagues in the old Creative Services Department of *The Buffalo News*, especially fellow authors Lyndsey D'Arcangelo and Maria Pascucci, for reminding me that it's never too late to chase your dreams!

Chapter One
Ronnie vs. Mother Nature

As a baseball player, little Ronnie had no business being anywhere near a diamond. He wasn't at all athletic. In fact, think about all those sports movies like the *Bad News Bears* that always have one kid who just plain looks out of place on an athletic field. Well, that was Ronnie.

I had to be around 11 years old at the time, and first base was my regular position. I have no idea why ... as I was always one of the shorter players on the team. But I could hold my own at first base. On a team called "Nova Nine" — named because there were nine of us and because our coach drove a beat up old Nova — having someone who could catch a ball at first base was quite an accomplishment. We were the real life version of those lovable Bad News Bears from the big screen.

Our time together as a team lasted a couple of years. We won a total of one game. It was against my cousin's team. We may have been horrible, but at least I retained family bragging rights.

Back to little Ronnie. Ronnie was always a sickly shade of white and appeared to weigh about as much as a Louisville Slugger. He was the kid who always had a runny nose. It could have been sunny and 85 degrees, and that nose was running like a faucet. And of course, we did what all boys do. We picked on him.

But every dog has its day, and so did Ronnie.

We were playing at the local ballpark in a steady rain. The infield had turned to mud, and puddles had formed all around the base paths. Somehow, Ronnie had made it to first base. It very well could have been the only at bat all season where he actually made it to a base. But there he was, on first, wiping the rain off his face just like the rest of us.

One ground ball later and Ronnie suddenly found himself standing on second base, an accomplishment that none of us, including Ronnie, could believe. But there he was, a smile stretched across his face. There had to be one nervous little guy hiding behind the smile and snot.

And then fate took over. The next batter hit the water-logged baseball right back up the middle. Splat! The ball found a puddle in centerfield and stopped dead in its tracks. Ronnie was encouraged to run to third base, and he did, slipping and stumbling all the way, being extra cautious not to fall into any of the rapidly expanding puddles. At the same time, the right fielder, closest to the stopped ball, struggled to find a handle on the slippery baseball. That was all we needed to give Ronnie the green light to head home.

You could see every emotion in Ronnie's face: surprise, shock, disbelief. But there he was, rounding third and heading toward home, his drenched sneakers in a desperate search for traction on the muddy base path. "He's going to make it! Ronnie's going to score a run," we all thought, simultaneously rising from the bench to cheer him on.

Only one problem. Standing in the way of Ronnie and his first run of the year was the biggest puddle on the field, a long and deep puddle that ran pretty much from third to home. Ronnie appeared to being hydroplaning most of the way, with the mud sucking at his sneakers with every step he took.

About midway through that puddle, Ronnie's feet shot out sideways and down he went, face first into the watery mess. Mud and water was dripping from every inch of his body as he tried, unsuccessfully, to stand.

We, the teammates who always enjoyed making fun of Ronnie, were suddenly all standing within just a few feet of him, loudly encouraging him to forget about the rain, the water, the mud ... and whatever his parents might say to him during the car ride home. We wanted just one thing, and that was for Ronnie to arrive at home plate before the sloppy ball made its way to the awaiting catcher.

Knowing that getting back up on his feet was improbable at best, Ronnie started crawling toward home plate through the cold, muddy water. More stumbles occurred along the way. From the bench area to the base path, we, his teammates, were jumping up and down and shouting our encouragement. After what seemed like an eternity, the ball was finally making its way back to the catcher. Here comes Ronnie. Here comes the ball.

"Safe!" yelled the umpire as Ronnie reached for the plate with his right hand just prior to the ball's arrival in the catcher's mitt. You'd have thought Nova Nine had just beaten the New York Yankees in Game 7 of the World Series! We embraced Ronnie with a greeting so loud, so exciting, that all of us on the field probably still remember it to this day. I recall a good part of it like it was yesterday.

Ronnie had indeed scored a run. We lost the game, of course, but Ronnie had not only reached base but had actually scored, getting the best of Mother Nature in the process.

We treated Ronnie differently from that moment on. Suddenly, he was one of us. His determination to make it through the rain and mud — crawling on his belly the last 15 feet or so, was legendary!

I often think about Ronnie, more so than any other player on that unspectacular Nova Nine team. I wonder what he's doing today? I wonder if baseball is still a part of his life, like it is in mine?

Chapter Two
Player of the Game

We flash forward roughly 30 years or so. Now my son Andrew is about 11 and I'm coaching his baseball team. We're not as bad as Nova Nine, but we weren't very good either. We weren't too bad defensively, but it seemed that the entire team struggled to hit the ball on even a fairly regular basis.

On the team was a very shy, slight-of-frame little boy named John, who in several ways reminded me of little Ronnie from my boyhood days. While he appeared to have some medical problems that kept his physical development a notch or two behind the other boys on the team, he always worked very hard to overcome them. Like the other boys on the team, John always received an equal share of the playing time because that's just the way I coached. Every family had to pay the same amount to have their boy play in the town league. His family came to our games to cheer him on just like the other boys' families. So even though John struggled with the game, he still received an equal amount of playing time.

We won a few games during the year, but this game was not going to be one of them. We were playing the best team in the league, a team filled with little all-stars and guided by coaches who possessed that win-at-all-costs mentality. Hard as we may try, we weren't going to beat this team.

Before the game, I casually mentioned to the opposing coach that I had a boy with some minor physical issues. I did this so that he might have his pitchers take it a little easier on John during his turns at bat. Much to my surprise, the other coach thought that would be a good idea and indeed told his pitchers to take a little speed off the old fastball when John was standing at the plate.

But John's heroics that day would not be at the plate, but on the field. Left field, to be exact.

It was fairly late in the game and the score, as I had expected, wasn't very close. Stepping up to the plate for the opposition was their best player, a boy who, during the season, probably had as many home runs as my entire team had hits. He was a natural, possessing a great swing and all-around baseball ability that would surely land him a spot on the high school team in a couple of years.

He stepped to the plate with that usual look of confidence filling his eyes. In came the pitch. Whack! The ball took off like it was shot from a cannon. Its destination? Left field.

Much to my surprise, John got a pretty good read on the ball and started backpedaling almost immediately. His head still facing home plate but looking high into the sky, John continued to step backward, his arms dangling at his side.

I'm sure everyone at the ballpark was thinking the same thing ... here comes another trip around the bases. I could have had my best player out there in left field, and that ball wasn't going to be caught. No way, no how. I, for one, had seen this scenario unfold plenty of times before.

But little John had a surprise up his sleeve that day. He continued to move backward as quickly as his feet would carry him, and at the very last possible moment, his left arm and hand shot skyward as he reached up as high as he possibly could with his gloved hand. The screeching ball stuck in the webbing like an eight ball hit soundly into the corner pocket of a billiards table.

Both teams, the coaches and all the parents and spectators stopped for a split second in total disbelief. When reality took over, the place erupted in cheers from both sidelines. Players and coaches on both teams greeted John with high fives and slaps on the back. Even the young man who had just crushed the ball left the field with a big smile on his face. What an amazing moment ... one that would compete with any Top 10 highlight one might witness on ESPN.

John was always one of my favorite players, and he's grown into a fine young man. He graduated from the local high school in the top 15 of his class and now attends a private college in Buffalo where he reportedly excels at a different sport — table tennis. He'll never play left field for a major league baseball team, but it wouldn't shock me at all if some day he's running a successful Fortune 500 company, helping to send rockets into space or finding a cure for cancer.

And in his dorm room at college, a decade later, sits the ball from that game boasting the fading words, "Player of the Game."

Chapter Three
The Day it All Came Together
... Finally

Some people look at coaching youth sports as a chore. I never felt that way. In fact, I would say that it was a labor of love for me, and that's why I coached youth baseball for roughly a dozen years. On top of that, I served as president of our town's baseball league for three years and on its board of directors for a total of seven years. For the most part, it was an enjoyable and rewarding experience.

For the most part. My only major problem was with assistant coaches (not mine ... they were great). Typically, they don't want the responsibility that goes along with being the head coach, but "for the most part" they feel entitled to act like fools and yell at players, umpires and board members because of the "assistant coach" title. I truly believe that the world, yes, the world, would be a far better place without assistant coaches.

The best part of coaching, for me, was dealing with the kids. Helping them to develop their athletic skills was challenging and fun, but it was more important to me that they develop into well-rounded, respectful young adults. I tried my best to keep the same group of players together, and was pretty successful in doing so. They weren't the most talented group of ballplayers, but they were great kids from excellent families. When you've got a supportive group of parents behind you, it's hugely advantageous.

Keeping the same players together for years did have its drawbacks, the biggest being that we just weren't that talented. In fact, we went through two levels of town baseball — Grasshoppers and Midgets — without ever posting a winning record. That's five seasons if you're keeping score at home.

Then things changed dramatically, and I remember the exact circumstances. It was our first year of "Junior" baseball (ages 13-15), and our first year on the regulation 90-foot diamonds. We were having a decent but unspectacular season. It was a cool Saturday morning and I had called a practice at one of the town's parks. It had rained the night before and there were a few puddles on the infield, but it wasn't bad enough to keep us from practicing. Ironically, it was the very same field where Ronnie had his memorable moment decades earlier.

Practice got off to a poor start and quickly went from bad to worse. It was one of those days; the boys just weren't listening and were giving a half-hearted effort at best. Balls hit to the infielders were being missed with regularity, and fly balls to the outfield were being dropped one after another. Finally, I had seen enough.

"Fine," I said in a very frustrated tone. "If you don't want to practice hard, then you can run." And run they did. "See that bench over there," I asked, pointing to the players' bench at another diamond off in the distance. "I want you to run — not jog — all the way around that bench and back here to our bench. And no shortcuts. If I see anyone cutting corners, you'll all do it again."

The boys groaned their displeasure but took off for the distant bench. They made it back one by one, huffing and puffing quite hard, and were quickly directed to our bench. When all were gathered, I chewed them out for a good 10 minutes. I used all the cliches in the book — don't waste my time ... if you don't want to be here, then quit ... when you're here I need to see 100 percent effort all the time. And with that, I sent them back to their positions on the diamond.

I walked to the plate with a big aluminum bat in hand. My displeasure with the boys was reflected in my swing, the bat letting out a loud "PING" when I made contact with the ball. I swung the bat harder each time, just waiting for the first mistake or lazy attempt so I could yell at them again.

For the remainder of practice, the boys were completely focused on baseball. They stopped ground balls that I would have been afraid to get in front of. They made running catches on long fly balls. Their throws to the bases were chest high and 100 percent accurate. They backed each other up just in case ... but they didn't miss a ball! My son Andrew was stationed at second base. I hit a hard grounder up the middle, and he dove to his right to make the play. His dive took him directly into one of the larger infield puddles. He didn't say a word. Just made the stop, got to his feet, and quickly and accurately threw the ball to first.

Normally, a teammate falling into a puddle would have resulted in uncontrollable laughter from the team. But not this time. Andrew didn't complain. His teammates didn't laugh. They all just stood at the ready, watching my bat to see in which direction the next ball would be hit. They were completely focused, and nothing was going to get them off their game.

Following practice, I had them all sit down again on the bench where I had earlier chewed them out for their lack of effort. This time I gushed with praise. It was the effort and commitment that every coach dreams about. The boys were tired but I could sense that they were proud of their performance. I knew that they had it in them. Deep down, they knew it too.

It was at this practice that they became a "team." Throughout the remainder of the season I frequently reminded them of that Saturday morning practice and of the fact that they could be excellent ballplayers if they could bring out that focus and commitment during games.

We went on to post our very first winning season. For the first time ever, it was on to the playoffs!

Chapter Four
Championship Saturday

In the West Seneca Youth Baseball Association, "Championship Saturday" was a major event. Not only did all of our divisions play their championship games at our main park — Centennial Field — it was also the day of our league picnic. I was still president of the league that year, so there was a lot to do in addition to coaching my son's team. We had about 700 trophies to hand out and about 1,500 mouths to feed. It was a daylong event and it required a lot of hard work on behalf of the league's board of directors ... but it was fun for everyone — the players, coaches, friends, families and spectators.

We had the early game, a 9 a.m. start, I believe. We were set to play a pretty talented team with a couple of good pitchers, including a big right-hander and a lanky lefty with an unusual windup and, at times, some pretty nasty stuff. But I was confident. Since that fateful Saturday morning practice, my team had been playing exceptionally well.

The game was close throughout. After six innings of this scheduled seven-inning affair, we clung to a hard-fought 6-4 lead. Fortunes would quickly turn, however, in the top of the seventh. Our pitching started to fall apart. I had to bring in Brandon, one of our practice pitchers — who had never pitched in a real game for me — with the bases loaded in the top of the seventh. He allowed the lead run to score but otherwise worked out of an incredibly difficult situation. We headed to the bottom of the seventh inning now trailing by a 7-6 score.

After a quick pep talk in the dugout, I headed to my usual spot in the coach's box along third base. I saw my mother and brothers sitting in the bleachers. I knew they were there, but I hadn't paid much attention to the growing crowd. As I stood alongside third base ready to send signals to the batter, I took notice of the now massive crowd. The bleachers on both sides of the diamond were filled to capacity. Spectators in lawn chairs sat in rows behind the massive backstop. Countless people stood shoulder to shoulder along the fences leading down both the right and left field lines.

We were accustomed to seeing a handful of familiar faces at our games, usually a few parents and maybe a friend or two. By the last inning of this championship game between a bunch of hard-playing mostly 13 and 14 year olds, there had to be 500 or so people on hand to witness the outcome. I was impressed that my boys remained focused on the prize at hand.

The inning started with Dave, one of our better hitters, coming to the plate. He quickly stroked a single and one out later was standing next to me at third base. Joey was up next. He wasn't great at the plate, but when he gets on base, just try to stop him! Joey could give a jackrabbit a run for its money. He was by far the fastest player on our team, and quite possibly the best baserunner in the league. If stealing bases was a crime, he'd still be serving time.

A wild pitch allowed Dave to score the tying run and Joey, my assistant coach's son, to reach first base. That would bring Tom to the plate. Just two pitches later and Joey the jackrabbit was standing next to me at third base. I told you he was fast!

Tom would walk and then take second. I told him he didn't need to move an inch, that his run didn't matter. I didn't want him to get caught up in some freakish double-play situation or, God forbid, picked off.

Next up? You guessed it, my son Andrew. It was every coach's dream and nightmare at the same time. Joey was bouncing all over at third base, almost uncontrollable. Nothing was going to stop him from scoring. Tom, not known for his running skills, stood dutifully on second base. The boys and coaches in both dugouts stood at the top of the stairs. The crowd was abuzz. I could hear my brothers, my wife Maureen and daughter Lauren all shouting encouragement to Andrew from the bleachers.

Like most of his teammates, Andrew wasn't a great hitter. He was pretty good at drawing a walk, and for some odd reason he got hit by pitch an awful lot. I sometimes think it was the opposing players and coaches getting back at me for something, as I was a fairly no-nonsense league president. But it never really bothered Andrew. He would just shrug it off, head to first base and show me the bruise when we got home.

So here he was standing at the plate with hundreds of eyes upon him. He's facing the lanky lefty reliever who had been unusually wild to this point. But with one out and the winning run standing on third, his control started to return. He jumped ahead of Andrew with a one ball, two strike count. On deck was a player who started the season very strong at the plate but had been ice cold the second half of the season. If Andrew didn't make contact, I was expecting extra innings.

When Andrew is swinging properly, he hits a lot of balls right up the middle of the field. I was praying for one of those hits. Here comes the pitch. Andrew takes a good swing and makes contact off the very end of the bat. The ball is heading up the middle.

It seems like the play occurs in slow motion. Joey breaks for home. Tom stays put on top of second base. The ball rolls past the pitcher's mound. The second baseman dives to his right. Simultaneously, the shortstop dives to his left. The center fielder is charging hard toward the infield. The ball barely makes it to the outfield grass. Joey crosses home plate with his arms raised high into the air. Andrew crosses first base and is quickly mobbed by his teammates.

I stay calm and walk slowly off the field.

Well, that's not exactly accurate.

In reality, I was probably the most excited person on the field ... perhaps the most excited person in the world at that very moment, jumping up and down and racing to join the celebration over at first base. It wasn't because my son had just won the game with a seeing-eye single that sent Joey home with the winning run, but because of everything these boys overcame to win a championship. All the practices, the determination, the perseverance, the hard work. Remember, this is a team that had never had a winning season before.

Now we were league champions, and no one could ever take that away from us. People I had never met before were coming up to me and Andrew all afternoon to congratulate us. It was, by far, the highlight of my coaching career. I didn't want that day to end!

Before I could return to the business of running a picnic and handing out trophies, I had one more piece of business to take care of on the infield. At the end of the championship game, it's tradition for both teams to line up along the base paths to receive their championship game medals. Our opponents received their silver medals first, and each boy receiving his award also received a loud and well-deserved ovation from the remaining crowd.

And then it was my turn to place gold medals around the necks of my championship team. Handshakes with the players turned into heartfelt hugs. I choked back tears as I presented each and every medal to the players and then to my assistant coaches. The parents of the players all stood in line behind the boys. I can assure you that I wasn't the only one with tears in my eyes.

Chapter Five
In Stitches

Another long Western New York winter had just ended and an absolutely gorgeous Saturday was upon us. It was a sure sign that it was indeed time to perform that annual spring ritual that awaits so many of us homeowners. Yes, it was time to clean out the garage.

Sure, my garage is packed with the typical things one would expect to find in the average suburban homeowner's garage ... tools, hoses, bicycles, sports equipment, empty soda bottles and a wide assortment of odds and ends. But there's something else you need to know about my garage before you can get an accurate picture. In the back of our attached garage is a doggy door, large enough for Rudy, our 100-plus pound Golden Retriever, to squeeze his massive and muscular frame through whenever he needed to find relief in our fenced-in yard. Now picture an unusually muddy yard that's gone through countless freeze cycles over the course of fall, winter and now spring. The result: a garage floor that was covered in mud (and probably a few other surprises), and a heavy coating of dust and Rudy hair upon everything else.

In a nutshell, spring cleaning the Kirchmyer garage was no simple task. Everything had to be carried or dragged out to the driveway and washed or wiped down, and the combination of mud and Golden Retriever hair scraped from the floor.

While going through a basket full of sports equipment, I came across an old baseball glove. Having coached youth baseball for a number of years, I had lots of equipment stored in the garage. This glove, however, was a little unusual and I have no idea where it came from. It was pretty old — a Steve Garvey model. Ironically, I would later meet Mr. Garvey at the Buffalo Bisons baseball team's annual fantasy camp, and once again in Las Vegas a couple of years later.

But back to the garage, where I examined the Garvey glove for quite awhile. I always enjoyed sports memorabilia, and had a small collection of autographed merchandise at the time. As the garage once again began to look more like a garage than a den for some filthy wild animal, I thought it might look pretty cool if I attached the Garvey glove to one of the interior walls of the garage, and slowly surround it with gloves featuring the names of other baseball players worthy enough of having their name stamped on leather.

My daughter Lauren, who was around eight or nine at the time, had dancing classes that Saturday and would arrive home later in the afternoon with a friend in tow ... another Lauren. I showed the old baseball glove to the Laurens, and told them my idea of lining the garage walls with similar gloves "autographed" by famous players. They seemed somewhat interested in my story, but were ready to embark on an adventure of their own. One of the neighbors down the street was having a big garage sale, and the girls were chomping at the bit to go check it out.

Down the street they went without a care in the world, all the way chattering about dancing, or school, or whatever it is that cute little girls chatter about. A few minutes later they came running back to our house, breathless and excited.

"Dad, there's an old baseball glove at the garage sale and it has a name on it," my Lauren announced. "Who's name," I inquired. They didn't know. But it was written in script and it was in pretty good condition.

"How much do they want for it," I asked. "One dollar," my daughter replied.

So I pulled a dollar from my wallet and sent the girls back to the garage sale to purchase this found treasure that I would surely add to my garage wall. They ran back down the street to the neighbor's house, making sure they would arrive there before anyone else decided they needed an old one-dollar baseball glove.

Mission accomplished! The Laurens made their purchase and came running

back to our house once again, where I
greeted them in the garage. "Let's see
what we have here," I said to them, a
little excited myself, I must admit.

I took the glove from the Laurens and
examined it closely, turning it over to
check both the front and back. But that's
odd. I didn't see a signature. So I
examined it again, a little more carefully
the second time. Still, no sign of any
signature.

"I thought you said this glove had a
signature, like the Steve Garvey glove," I
said to the Laurens. "It does," both girls
replied.

"Where" I asked. "Can you show
me?"

And they did. Pointing to script
lettering up the side of one of the
fingers. I read the words aloud.

"Nylon Stitched."

Of course, I couldn't contain my
laughter. My dear, sweet daughter and
her friend had just bought me a baseball
glove — to be showcased forever on my
garage wall, or so they thought —
autographed by the immortal "Nylon
Stitched."

It was a classic father-daughter moment that I'll never forget, probably because I still love to tell the story even a decade later. Lauren just rolls her eyes every time she hears me retelling the tale, still slightly embarrassed by her mistake. But I think she also enjoys the fact that she's the star of one of her dad's all-time favorite stories!

Chapter Six
Bump(er)s & Bruises

While it's a family favorite, baseball isn't the only sport ever played by our family. Maureen and I always let the kids try any sport they wanted to. After sampling several, Lauren stuck with softball for several years and dance, which she started at the age of three and continues today. In fact, she's currently minoring in dance at college and would like to perhaps open her own studio one day, travel the world with a performance group or write for a dance magazine.

A quick aside about dancing: it's the most expensive activity known to man. Lauren dances competitively, and she's in roughly 10 to 12 dances per year. So that means that you pay for classes, a costume for each dance, and a wide variety of shoes and other essentials like leotards and makeup. There are competition fees and travel expenses as well. Maureen pays all the dancing bills. I figure we've already paid the equivalent of a college education. But Lauren loves it, so how do you possibly say no? Answer: You don't.

Andrew would ultimately decide on baseball during the warmer months and bowling during fall and winter right up through his high school years. But there was a two-year experiment with ice hockey that started when he was five years old and resulted in zero goals but plenty of laughs. He even got to play briefly between periods of a Buffalo Sabres game at Buffalo's old War Memorial Auditorium. Ironically, it was the closest he ever came to scoring a goal, missing the puck by just a whisker as it slid past the opposing goalie and into the net.

As I mentioned, he stuck with it for two seasons. Two seasons of early practices, lacing up skates, lugging equipment and hanging out in chilly ice rinks and cramped locker rooms with fanatical hockey parents.

Andrew didn't have a scorer's touch or a killer instinct. In fact, he could barely keep his balance on those skates. But he was the best waver on the team. As the other boys would rush up and down the ice in pursuit of the puck, Andrew would leisurely skate past the stands and wave to us in the crowd. It was very cute. The other parents thought so too and would laugh and wave back at Andrew every time he passed by. He was a star, just not in a hockey sense.

No, hockey just wasn't in his blood. On a positive note, he played two full seasons and never suffered an injury. Never got whacked by a puck or a stick. Never struck his head hard on the ice during one of his frequent falls. Never even a scratch, come to think of it.

So when Andrew announced that he was done with hockey and wanted to try bowling, we were pleased. The local bowling alley had a bumper bowling league on Saturday mornings. Bumper bowling is just like real bowling, only they put these big bumpers in the gutters so that newcomers to the game aren't frustrated by constantly throwing gutter balls.

Best of all, bumper bowling had a set time every Saturday morning. No traveling in the dark to frigid ice rinks anymore. No crazy expenses. It was something like $5 per week and you could use their bowling balls and shoes. Perfect!

The very first week of bumper bowling, Maureen got his bowling shoes from the counter while I helped him find a lightweight ball that would fit his hand. We pointed him in the direction of the pins and I sat down to read my Saturday morning newspaper. Life was good.

A few minutes later Andrew comes running up to me holding his hand and starting to cry. He had gotten his fingers pinched between two balls on the ball return.

"Toughen up," I told him. "Don't worry about it. You'll be fine." And with that, I pointed him back to the lane and went back to my newspaper.

Later that day, Maureen, Andrew, Lauren and I would go out for dinner and a movie. During dinner, Andrew would make an unexpected announcement.

"Look at my finger," he said proudly, holding it high above the table. Maureen and I both took a quick glance and were shocked by what we saw before us ... a swollen finger all shades of black, blue, purple and red.

"How did that happen" we asked immediately, our voices reflecting our concern. Andrew reminded us that his finger had been pinched between two bowling balls earlier in the day. My mind raced back to that moment and the fact that I simply shrugged off his injury with a command to "toughen up." I felt horrible. We paid the tab and headed quickly to the nearest immediate care center.

A doctor examined the injury and felt it was bad enough to require an X-ray. Fortunately, the X-ray came back negative and nothing was broken. The doctor applied a splint to the badly bruised finger and told us to monitor it closely for a couple of days, but that he would be fine, which he was. Still, I felt like I had failed "Parenthood 101."

Two years of hockey and not a scratch. One day of bumper bowling and it's off to the emergency room. Go figure.

Chapter 7
Pray for Us!

Church league softball. Just saying the words brings visions of friendly competition, lots of high-fives between players on both teams, scores of spectators exchanging pleasantries and a group prayer at the end of the game. Then, it's off to the pot luck social in the school hall and everyone's invited!

Now picture the exact opposite, and you have the West Seneca Church League in its prime. We hated each other ... the coaches, the players, the umpires. No one escaped the wrath of the Church League players.

Don't believe me? Allow me to share some examples of our unsportsmanlike conduct, for which I'm sure we'll all pay dearly in the afterlife.

Our team was sponsored by the Knights of St. John at St. Bonaventure Church, where I was a parishioner from birth to age 40. I attended elementary school there, helped out in the rectory on Sunday mornings, and was baptized, confirmed and married there. Both of our children were also baptized there.

Our team was the laughing stock of the league for many years. The bright yellow uniforms certainly didn't help, and only brought more attention to our sad play on the field. Competitive we were not.

Eventually, as the older players went into softball retirement, we replaced them with some talented ballplayers. Soon we were not only competitive, but battling for league championships every year. At one point we won several consecutive titles and even recorded the rare undefeated season.

In our very first championship game we were trailing late in the game by six or seven runs. We were playing our most hated rival, and it was pretty apparent that we weren't going to win the game. I was pitching and Gary, who to this day remains my catcher after 20-plus years — failing knees and all — was working behind the plate.

Following a hit by a player from the opposing team, Gary picked up the player's bat and flung it into the backstop. He said he was just clearing it out of the way, but I knew better. So did the umpire, who wasted no time in kicking my frustrated catcher out of the game.

I was also the coach of the team at the time and felt it necessary to voice my displeasure with the ump. Our conversation, mostly one-sided and with me doing most of the talking, included more than a few colorful words. In my defense, some of those words — like jackass — can be found in the Bible. And this was the Church League after all.

It didn't take long for me to get tossed from the game as well. But before I left, I had to rearrange the fielders and call on a new pitcher and catcher, and that took a few minutes. The umpire, tired of waiting, told me to hurry things up, which set me off into another round of verbal abuse.

Now red-faced and with steam ready to burst from his ears, the veteran umpire looked straight at me, gave me the full action heave-ho and announced at the top of his lungs, "Now you're REALLY out of here!!!" It was the first time I had ever been kicked out of a game ... twice.

Over the years I witnessed firsthand several bench-clearing brawls, an opposing shortstop throwing dirt into the face and eyes of one of my teammates as he slid into second base, a first baseman on my team intentionally spiked and sent to the hospital for major foot repairs, two broken noses and an assortment of other antics that the big guy upstairs surely frowned upon.

And then there was the day I witnessed one of the funniest moments in Church League softball history. We were playing one of our rivals, of course, and they had two brothers who loved to get under the umpire's skin. They were chirping and complaining the entire game, insisting that all of the calls were going against them. The simple fact of the matter was that we had a much better team at the time, and we were winning this game quite handily. Their frustration was very apparent.

Finally, the ump reached his breaking point. He called timeout and gave the brothers one final warning. "One more word from either of you and you'll be gone," the umpire warned.

Just minutes later, my friend Don came to the plate. Don was a decent hitter and didn't take kindly to making an easy out, which he did this time. As Don walked back to our bench, the umpire turned his back for just a moment. It was all the time that Don needed to launch his bat all the way into right field. The spinning projectile cleared the first baseman by a good 15 feet, but landed silently in the soft outfield grass.

That set off the two brothers who had been previously warned by the umpire to keep their mouths shut. They both went into a rant, and the umpire stopped them dead in their tracks, throwing both out of the game ... and out of the park for good measure. In the meantime, during all of the commotion around the umpire, one of our players quickly ran out to right field to retrieve the bat that Don had thrown in anger. With no evidence to convict him, Don was allowed to stay in the game.

It's probably the only time in softball history that a player's bat-throwing temper tantrum got two opponents thrown out of a game. We still laugh about it.

Looking back on our Church League days, I find it hard to believe that anyone would want to umpire those games. I hope they were paying those guys a lot of money, but I doubt it.

Eventually, the Church League began to evolve into a bar league, and ironically, the games evolved as well, becoming less life or death and just a little friendlier. One season near the end of our run in that league, we were still listed as St. Bonaventure on the schedule, but were actually being sponsored by a local beer distribution company that provided us with Coors baseball shirts.

Before one Tuesday evening game, a confused umpire approached our diamond. "Is this the Church League?" he asked me. "Yes, it is," I replied. "Then who the hell are you ... Saint Coors?"

I chuckled at his observation. It's no wonder he had that confused look on his face.

Chapter 8
Down and Out!

One of the scariest Church League moments is one that we now look back on and laugh about every time it's mentioned ... which happens to be several times a year.

We were playing on a less-than-spectacular softball diamond on school grounds not far from my house. It was the typical schoolyard scene with three closely placed softball diamonds, tennis courts, a basketball court and the obligatory rusting playground equipment. That was back in a time long ago when playground equipment was actually made of metal. And after a few years that metal would rust. We'd still play on it despite the cuts and scratches. And you know what? We all lived to tell about it! None of that plastic and resin and wood chip stuff that they call a playground today.

Anyway, it was an evening game and, as usual, I was pitching and my pal Gary was catching. It was a pretty competitive league; the pitchers could throw pretty hard and both stealing and bunting were allowed. It was played just like regular baseball.

The umpires back then all had a nickname. Daily game schedules were printed in our local newspaper, along with the nickname of the umpire assigned to each game. Our game was assigned to a guy called "Motor." He was a decent umpire, and we had no problems with him over the years that I can recall. Let's put it this way: He never kicked me or Gary out of a championship game, so he was cool.

Motor carried that nickname because he would always ride his motorcycle to the game and park it right behind the backstop, perhaps for a quick getaway should one of our famous Church League bench-clearing brawls get too far out of hand.

So here we were, playing a game with Motor serving as our umpire. He would always take his position behind the pitcher, not behind the catcher. That never happens today. All of our umpires now report for duty behind home plate. After this game, however, I'm sure Motor considered moving behind the plate like the other umpires, or perhaps giving up his part-time gig completely.

Gary is a good catcher. We've played together for so many years that it's like we can read each other's minds when we're on the field. We often use head movements to communicate — high and tight, low and outside. He knows what it means, for example, if I touch my right leg with my fingers or tap my left leg with my glove. It's definitely an advantage that we have over the batters.

What Gary doesn't have is an accurate arm. Throwing runners out at second was never his specialty. Motor would learn that lesson the hard way.

I don't remember who we were playing that day, the score, the inning of "the incident" or the exact count, but I do remember that our opponents had a man on first who was attempting to steal second base. You never knew where the ball was going to end up when Gary tried to throw out a runner. Sometimes the ball hit its mark, quickly finding its way into the glove of the awaiting second baseman or shortstop. Just as often it would end up somewhere in the outfield or coming straight at me, causing me to catch it midway on its flight to second so that I would not be injured.

To recap the scenario: Man at first. I pitch the softball to Gary and the runner at first base takes off for second. Gary comes up throwing. Seeing what's happening, Motor turns around and takes a few steps toward shortstop so he can get a good view of the play that's about to occur at second base. His back is now facing Gary.

SPLAT!

Stunned silence. Everyone is in shock it seems, too afraid to even move. Motor is lying face down in the dirt right in front of the shortstop, midway between second and third base. Gary's throw was, you might say, off its mark. That ugly "splat" sound was the ball hitting Motor square in the back of his head. We slowly made our way over to him to see if he was, well, still alive.

For several minutes, Motor stayed on the ground moaning and obviously in a lot of pain. The poor guy, he didn't know what hit him. Ironically, I can't recall if Motor recovered enough to finish the game or even if he was able to hop on his motorcycle and ride it home or to the nearest emergency department.

But wait. The story doesn't end there.

The following week we're scheduled to play at the very same schoolyard diamond and Motor is once again assigned to handle our game. We wondered if he'd show up at all. Honestly, he could have been dead or in the hospital recovering from serious head trauma for all we knew. And if he did show up, would he hold last week's incident against us?

A few minutes before the game, we hear the familiar rumble of Motor's motorcycle heading toward the diamond. He was indeed alive, and looking rather healthy I might add.

As we're on the field before the game, Motor approached Gary, who was in the process of receiving my warm-up pitches.

"How you doing," Gary asked Motor, afraid of what his answer might be. "Great," the umpire replied. "But you should have seen what happened to me last week. The catcher was trying to throw out a guy at second and hit me in the back of the head."

"No kidding ..." Gary replied.

Motor had no idea that it was Gary who had inadvertently knocked him senseless just a week earlier with his errant throw. And since he was going to umpire our game that night, we weren't about to break that news to him.

Chapter 9
Bottom of the Ninth

Before we move on to other sporting topics, there are a few more baseball and softball stories that I feel the need to share. Individually, they probably don't warrant their own chapters, but together they wrap up the diamond antics rather nicely.

I'll start with a bat story. Not a baseball bat, but a bat of the winged variety.

Now I've seen timeouts called for a variety of reasons, some even involving animals. Over the years we've had numerous games stopped due to a dog or dogs running onto the field. I even remember a game or two that stopped momentarily while we chased geese off the field. But bats?

We were playing a night game at a local park and dusk was settling in. The large lights surrounding the diamond went on, drawing a swarm of insects to each of the light posts. I was standing on first base at the time, waiting for the opposing pitcher to throw his next pitch, when a rather large bat came swooping across the field, cutting a jagged path about 10 feet off the ground right between me and the pitcher.

The bat, looking only for his next meal, scared the living daylights out of me! Stunned by the suddenness of its arrival, I did what anyone else would do. I shouted "TIME OUT ... BAT!!!"

Not everyone had seen the bat making its mad dash above the infield, and most of the players, including the umpire, must have thought I had ... gone batty.

Honestly, it was a funny story ... but maybe of the you-had-to-be-there variety.

***

My daughter Lauren was playing town softball and I was coaching first base for her team. She was playing at a well-kept grouping of diamonds surrounded by fields. Out of the corner of my eye I could see what appeared to be a low but quick moving cloud. Actually, that cloud would turn out to be a huge swarm of bees, and they flew just a few feet over our heads.

Fortunately, they were here and gone in less than 30 seconds, and apparently had no interest in the game or, even better, stinging any of the participants!

***

One year I had a roster opening on Andrew's baseball team and selected a boy who I wasn't familiar with. All I knew is what I read on his baseball application. What stuck out was his size. A teenager, he was just four feet, six inches tall.

But Jesse turned out to be a player ... tough as nails. In fact, I remember playing him at second base during the late innings of a playoff game. We had a very slim lead at the time, and the other team had men at first and second with only one out. The runner at second was taking a generous lead, so Jesse had to hold him on. Sure enough, the batter hits a scorcher toward second base.

Jesse quickly tried to get back into position, but there was no way he was going to get his glove around in time. So he stuck his hand out — the one without the glove — barehanded the fast-approaching grounder off a hop, and quickly tossed it to our shortstop who stepped on second for the force and then threw on to first to complete an inning-ending double play.

It was an amazing play and I ran toward Jesse and rewarded him with a leaping chest bump. I think it made his season to see his coach so excited!

I'll also remember Jesse for a great adjustment he made at the plate. He struck out quite a few times early in the season, overwhelmed a bit by the bigger pitchers. So I pulled him aside one day and convinced him to use his size to his advantage. "Go up and take a few pitches," I told him. "Walks are just as good as a hit. Go up there and get even smaller."

And so he did, crouching down just a little bit more than usual at the plate. His small strike zone practically disappeared, and the boy who seldom drew a walk the first half of the season drew 14 during the second half, helping the team advance through the playoffs and into the championship game and driving the opposing pitchers and coaches crazy in the process.

Jesse only played for me for that one season, and over the winter he had a growth spurt that brought him closer to par with the other boys. Regardless of his size, he was one tough little kid.

***

For three years running I was very fortunate to receive media credentials to attend Buffalo Bisons Fantasy Camp, an event that quickly became one of the highlights of summer for me. The Bisons are a AAA team and during those three years were the top farm club of the Cleveland Indians.

How many other people — excluding professional ball players, of course — can say they've played ball on the same field with Jack Clark, George Foster, Vida Blue, John Candelaria, Frank White, Dave Stewart, Mike LaValliere, Steve Garvey, Joe Niekro and Tippy Martinez? The highlight of those three years came when I hit a double to deep right field off of Blue. He had thrown me three consecutive knuckleballs and I was completely fooled on all three pitches but did manage to foul off the third one — just barely — to stay alive. I was praying he'd throw me something hittable, perhaps a fastball or a curve ... at least a pitch I had seen before! Sure enough, he tosses a batting practice fastball down the middle of the plate and I hit it right off the sweet spot. What a thrill!

The first year I attended camp, Joe Niekro was one of the pitchers the Bisons brought in for the event. He was getting up in age and spent a good portion of the day complaining about his feet. Anyway, before my first at bat I joked to my friend Don that I was going to line one right back up the middle and take Niekro down! I was joking, of course. I'm a pure pull hitter, typically hitting everything right down the line.

Wouldn't you know it, I take a hearty swing against Niekro and hit a bullet right up the middle. In an act of pure self-preservation, Niekro threw his glove in front of his face and deflected the ball away. Had he missed ... well, I don't even want to think about what might have happened! Needless to say, it probably would have been both my first and last invitation to Fantasy Camp.

Joe Niekro would pass away just a few months later. He was a very nice man and I'm glad I had a chance to meet him in person.

***

Talk about your scary moments. I'll never forget one practice I had called for Andrew's team when he was probably about 10 years old. There was the chance of a thunderstorm, but the day started sunny and bright and the team met at the appropriate diamond. About an hour into practice the storm clouds started rolling in and I decided to end things early. Lauren was with us that day — she loved to practice with Andrew's team — and we all hurried to pack the equipment bags and head to the car in an attempt to beat the rain.

The car was parked a good 200 yards from where we were practicing. As we started heading to the car, the winds suddenly turned violent and I could hear what sounded like a freight train bearing down on us. People who have experienced a tornado up close always say that it sounds just like a freight train. I told Andrew to run for the car. Carrying the heavy equipment bag in one arm, I scooped up Lauren with my free arm and also started running to the car. The noise we had heard, growing louder and louder as the weather approached, was caused by the biggest hail I had ever seen — roughly the size of large ice cubes. The sound we heard was the hail smacking rooftops, pavement, cars and anything in its path. After being pelted a couple of times, we all made it to the safety of the car. The hailstorm lasted several minutes, causing damage to numerous cars in the area. It was frightening!

By the time we arrived home the hail had stopped, but the evidence was left behind. We picked up several pieces and kept them in the freezer until Maureen arrived home. She hadn't heard about the storm and was sure that we were playing a trick on her. I don't think she really believed us until she saw a report on the local news about the damaging hail.

It was a sound unlike anything I've ever heard ... and one that I'll never forget.

***

Speaking of freaks of nature, Andrew still speaks of the day when we were practicing before one of his baseball games and a meteorite flew across the Western New York sky, leaving a flashy trail behind it. My back was to it so I missed the entire short-lived event, but Andrew assures me that it was quite spectacular. News reports had it landing somewhere in Pennsylvania.

***

The West Seneca Youth Baseball Association was hosting its very first baseball tournament, and we had a great turnout of teams for the weekend event. Saturday's games went off without a hitch, but the rains came on Sunday, washing out the championship games.

We were able to reschedule the games later in the week but had to change venues, instead playing at a local field that had lights for night games. Therefore, we decided to hold the championship games under the lights.

Just as the games began, a magnificent blimp came out of nowhere and hovered over the field. Believe me, this was totally unplanned, but the timing couldn't have been better. It turns out that the blimp was in town for a promotion of some kind, and its route took it right over our diamonds. And then, as dusk turned into darkness, a nearby shopping plaza had a huge fireworks display, with the show easily visible from the park that was hosting our games. People raved all night about the blimp and the fireworks display.

We certainly couldn't believe our luck, but were left to ponder how we were going to top such a performance next year. Fly-overs and fireworks just weren't in our league budget!

***

I strongly believe that participating in sports has addictive qualities: the more you play and the better you become, the more you need to play. That's the only way I can explain pitching a full seven-inning game just seven days after having my appendix removed. There's just no other logical explanation for that kind of stupidity.

Chapter 10
Revenge on the Racquetball Court

Those who know me fairly well know that I'm a pretty calm person. Sure, I've had my moments just like anyone else. I'll even admit there have been a few times during softball games that I might have intentionally thrown some "chin music," but that's part of the game, right?

Not that I've always been laid back. In my younger days, I could get a little excited during a sporting event. Hell, I could get angry just watching the Buffalo Bills or Buffalo Sabres on TV! But as we age, and have children who like to watch our every move and imitate our actions, we settle down emotionally. Good thing, I suppose.

But there was that one day on the racquetball court when I was pushed just a little too far. I played the sport for several years and was a pretty good "B" league player, even recording a couple of undefeated seasons. It was highly competitive and a great workout, one that would produce a full sweat after just a couple of minutes. Yes, the concrete walls and floors took their toll on my body, but what's wrong with running into a concrete wall when there's a point to be won?

Anyway, I was playing in a league match against a player who thought very highly of his skills. While most of the players in the league were what I would consider classy players, this guy was a grade A jerk. Always arguing points, always bringing up obscure rules ... you know the type.

So I'm playing this guy in a best of three match and I've got a pretty good lead. I'm controlling the game rather easily and giving him quite a workout in the process. He must not have liked it because he drilled me in the back with the ball.

I understand that getting hit is certainly part of the game, so I just brushed it off and resumed play. I, too, had accidentally hit a player or two during the season, so getting hit once was no big deal.

Then he hit me again. And again. And again and again and again and again and again.

Yep, he went on to hit me eight times in the span of nearly two games. By comparison, I had hit two people all season. And each time he hit me he wouldn't say a word. No "I'm sorry." No nothing.

I think the fact that there was no apology bothered me as much as getting hit. And while that ball might be made of soft rubber, it can hurt like hell when you're hit square in the back or in the neck area. A little apology was all I wanted.

Still nothing. He would just pick up the ball and head back to his spot on the court to line up for the next point.

I kept my cool and plotted my revenge. With the game and match already in hand, I returned one of his shots in a way that would require him to take position in the center of the court. He returned the shot and fell right into my trap, putting me in position for an easy forehand while standing just a few feet behind him. I wound up with all my might ...

WHAM! The ball flew from my racquet at lightning speed, reaching its target in a split second.

That target was the small of my opponent's back. He immediately dropped his racquet and grabbed at his back with both hands like he had just been stung by some highly venomous insect. Tears filled his eyes.

I remained silent ... just walked over and picked up the ball and returned to my spot on the court. Message delivered.

He was mad! The match ended a few points later and he complained about the hit all the way to the locker room and even the next time we played. But during our next contest he hit me just one time, and it was a glancing blow. Suddenly he became much more accurate with his shots. Amazing.

It was the one and only time that I intentionally hit another player on the racquetball court, but it has always stuck with me. I wonder if he played that way against other racquetball players? I wonder if he changed his game after receiving a taste of his own medicine?

I wonder if he still has a mark on the small of his back?

Chapter 11
Two That Didn't Get Away

As a boy, it was my dad who got me hooked on fishing. Sorry for the bad pun, but it's true. I remember him taking me and my brothers fishing at a local creek when we were all just pint-size. We weren't catching a lot of fish, but you could see them swimming just below the surface of the water. Nothing you'd want to eat, but to a kid, every fish is a trophy fish, regardless of size.

As my father was busy untangling lines and baiting hooks, I plucked a single blade of grass from the ground and dropped it into the water. The fish must have thought it looked appetizing, because two or three made a mad dash for it. Surely disappointed, they made a quick u-turn and dashed away. For some strange reason, I still remember that brief encounter with nature some four decades later.

So much has changed since then, especially the concept of "neighborhood." Today, suburban neighborhoods are all about square footage, perfectly manicured lawns and one-upping your neighbor's Christmas decorations. Come to think of it, we don't even see our neighbors all that much. After a hard day at work, people today come home and spend the remainder or their waking hours in front of the TV, sitting down at the family computer or perhaps enjoying their back yard retreat. And when winter arrives, forget it. Sighting a neighbor once the snow flies only seems to occur when you're both out plowing the driveway at night so you can get to work the next morning ... only to start the daily routine all over again.

That wasn't the case when I was a kid. The neighborhood that my older brothers and I grew up in was as spectacular as it was unspectacular. Unspectacular because the homes were tiny in terms of square footage, neighbors didn't compete with one another and everyone was like family. Garages were more a place for holding neighborhood parties than for holding cars, lawn mowers, bicycles and rusty old charcoal grills.

Our back yard backed up to a rather large field where we played baseball and football in the warmer months and hockey in the winter. It wasn't a park by any means, just an area cleared by the neighborhood adults who wanted a safe, nearby place where their kids could play relatively unsupervised. Our yard had a giant pear tree that produced delicious fruit every year, and I'd sit up in the branches and enjoy the occasional treat. In addition to the makeshift ball fields and hockey ponds just beyond our fence, there were countless forts built by the neighborhood kids, some of whom must have gone on to become skilled architects. Further back were the railroad tracks, where we'd frequently put things like pennies, nickels and stones on the tracks and be amazed by the spectacular results. And just beyond the railroad tracks were the remains of old orchards that continued to bear fruit every season. For a young boy, it was better than DisneyLand.

Within those fields were several ponds, all creatively named by the neighborhood children. There were two frog ponds, a small one before the railroad tracks and a larger one beyond the tracks. The larger of the two was home to some of the biggest bullfrogs you'll ever see. We would often try to catch them, but were successful on a very limited basis. We'd settle into a crouched position on the water's edge and sit as still as humanly possible until one of the massive bullfrogs would finally show its eyes from below the water's surface. We'd sit patiently as the frog revealed more and more of its body and then make a precision grab in hopes of catching our prey before it retreated deep into the murky water. Most days we'd come away empty handed ... and wet.

Twin ponds, surrounded by tall brush and chain linked fences, sat just a couple hundred yards further down the railroad tracks. The fences were meant to keep us out, but really, how often will a fence keep a group of boys with fishing poles and bait from their destination?

One of the ponds was called the Electric Pond, aptly named because of the tall towers that cast shadows upon the pond and carried scores of wires that no doubt provided the electricity for our entire neighborhood and several others. Sitting right next to it was the Vibrating Pond, which had an old dock that literally shook due to the immensely powerful voltage running above our heads. I'm sure it wasn't a safe environment to be in, hence the fence. And we never stayed there very long to fish, scared off by the wires and the thought that some person of authority would catch us and take us home to our parents.

Situated between the big Frog Pond and the grouping of the Electric and Vibrating ponds was the kid-friendly Turtle Pond, where I spent countless hours of my childhood with my trusty Zebco rod and reel. Well-stocked with a variety of fish, the Turtle Pond was also home to some snapping and non-snapping turtles, muskrats, geese and an assortment of nature's finest species. Worms worked great when you had them for bait, but chopped up pieces of hot dog or a small piece of rolled up white bread worked equally well for catching everything from Bluegill to bass to catfish.

When I was at the Turtle Pond, I always felt like Tom Sawyer on some type of great adventure ... which, of course, brings me to my most memorable Turtle Pond moment.

I was fishing with my cousin, and we were both about 10 years of age at the time. We hadn't been there long, and the fish were biting as usual. I took a fish off my hook, baited the hook again and cast the line back into the water. If you didn't have a bite within a minute, you'd quickly reel the line back in and try again. But this time, the line was stuck. Nothing ruined our fishing outings like a bad snag as we usually didn't carry extra hooks and sinkers with us. Snapping the line usually meant the end of fishing that day.

So I was very careful not to pull the snagged line too hard or stretch it beyond its limits. I moved side to side, taking the occasional backward step. Slowly, the snagged branch or whatever it was holding my hook under the water made its way closer to the shore. Whatever it was, it was heavy and was making the muscles in my arms ache.

I could tell by the amount of line that I had reeled in that my hook was within reach, so I pulled hard one more time to bring the unknown object to the surface and release my embedded hook.

And then, panic set in. What were we looking at? It wasn't a branch or a log at all. It was something truly strange. It looked prehistoric. Whatever it was, it scared the heck out of us! My cousin and I dropped our poles and sprinted all the way back home — over the railroad tracks, through the field, past the forts, and across the football field and baseball diamond. My father and brothers heard us yelling as we approached the fence.

Breathlessly, we tried to explain our unusual situation. We had caught some sort of prehistoric beast. It was huge! My father and brothers looked perplexed, but knew something must be wrong because we were truly panicked and had even run all the way home without our cherished fishing poles.

Not knowing what they were going to be up against, they grabbed the closest tools — a shovel and a large rake, I believe — and led us back to the Turtle Pond. We sheepishly followed ... several strides behind them.

We arrived back at the pond only to find that everything had returned to normal. Our poles sat side by side at the water's edge, and there was no evidence of the great beast. As my senses began to return, I was able to describe what I had seen coming from the water just a few minutes earlier. I vividly remembered the shape, the color, and the scaly skin.

There was no doubt about it. I had sunk my hook into the underside of a huge turtle. As I tugged and pulled the line, only a portion of its body penetrated the surface of the water. Maybe it was a leg or its tail, but it was massive. This had to be the great-grandfather of all those cute little turtles that we had seen so many times swimming across the surface of the pond. By the time we had returned with my father and brothers, the turtle had managed to escape and return to the water, no doubt as frightened as we were.

I returned to the Turtle Pond probably hundreds of times after that fateful day, but I never again spotted that massive turtle. Eventually, we started fishing again as if nothing had ever happened. The only unusual thing we'd catch after that was a massive catfish that measured well over a foot long, unusual even for the Turtle Pond.

The fishing gene would be passed down to my children, with Andrew always enjoying a fishing outing and a very young Lauren becoming famous for her baiting skills during a family vacation to a lake resort area a few hundred miles north of Toronto, Ontario. She wasn't that interested in fishing, but unlike all the other kids, she wasn't bothered at all when it came to putting a nightcrawler onto an awaiting hook. In fact, she took a great deal of pride in her strange talent.

The resort had a lot of daily activities for kids, and a fishing derby was part of the festivities. At the end of the week, the boy or girl with the biggest fish would earn the coveted fishing derby trophy, a nice little prize with a big, gold fish adorning the top. Andrew had his eye on that trophy all week, but he wasn't catching anything bigger than maybe seven inches off the docks.

Finally, on the last day of the contest, Andrew and I headed to one of the docks after a brief rain shower. Together, we cast our lines into the water. He was using a kiddie fishing pole of some sort. Suddenly there was a great splash in the water. Andrew had hooked a biggie. I turned around to see him pulling his fishing pole toward his chest with both hands, watching as the pole bent nearly in half under the weight of the fish. He struggled but managed to bring the fish out of the water and to the edge of the dock. I reached over and grabbed the line with one hand and his fish with the other ... just as the line snapped. It was a BIG bass. We could hardly contain our excitement.

Gripping the still thrashing fish with both hands, we made our way over to the main office where the official fishing derby measurements were kept. Andrew's fish came in at 15 inches, just big enough to win the weekly derby and earning him that prized trophy, which remains in his room to this day along with a photo of me, him and that big bass, which we returned to the lake after the official measurement.

But I'm afraid this story has a sad ending. After releasing the fish, I suddenly realized that I never removed the hook from its mouth. The line had snapped as Andrew was pulling the fish onto the dock, and amid all the excitement, I completely forgot about the hook. I don't think I ever told Andrew that part of the story.

Sorry, pal.

Chapter 12
Adventures of the
'Puckarattzi'

I'll credit my friend Don for coming up with a great idea ... using his love of sports to benefit local charities. Don has an impressive autograph collection, his pride and joy being the more than 1,000 autographed hockey pucks he's accumulated over the past couple of years. He attends alumni events, hangs out around arenas, chases visiting teams as they board the bus at their hotel. He's all over the place! I call him a "puckarattzi."

But Don's "stalking" of athletes has raised thousands of dollars for countless nonprofit organizations. When he sets his sights on an athlete, he'll bring not one puck, but several. If he gets more than one signed, he keeps one for his collection and the others in a separate collection that he donates to charity. If the charity needs items for a raffle or basket auction, Don donates a set of hockey pucks that, in the end, generate big bucks for the organization. He does the same with autographed baseballs, footballs ... you name it. If it has a signature on it, people love it and will bid on it.

Come to think of it, I have several friends with impressive sports collections. Tom, one of my former baseball players, has a collection of sports bobbleheads that exceeds well over 300. Another friend could open a sports museum tomorrow with his impressive collection. Seriously, if he had his collection on display in downtown Buffalo, for example, I'd pay to see it. It's that impressive.

My collection is very modest by comparison, featuring a handful of autographed pucks, baseballs, footballs, photos, books and a few other miscellaneous items. I don't have a lot of big name autographs ... mostly just players that I like or have some connection to.

Chasing autographs has become somewhat of a family hobby, as

Maureen often accompanies me on my adventures. We've been known to stand in line, sometimes for two hours, to get an autograph of a player we like. But there are two things I won't do ... I won't buy an autograph and I won't sell an autograph. Like Don, most of our extra autographed items are donated to some of our favorite charities and have raised thousands of dollars. It's truly a hobby we can feel good about!

One of my funniest and most memorable "puckarattzi" experiences happened in 2008 in nearby Rochester, N.Y. The American Hockey League's Rochester Americans were in their final year as the farm team of the Buffalo Sabres and Don had been asking me for several months to join him and his son Kenny on a road trip to chase some Sabres prospects as well as some prospects from the visiting team. So I checked out the Amerks website one day and noticed that they were having a team Hall of Fame induction ceremony near the end of the season. Two men with ties to the organization and the NHL, Craig Charron and Gates Orlando, were to be inducted. We circled the date on our calendars.

We headed to Rochester and arrived several hours prior to the Amerks game. Don, being a highly skilled puckarattzi, knew exactly where the Rochester players parked their cars, where the visiting team's bus would pull up and which doors the players would use to enter the arena. When we arrived, we noticed a note on the door regarding an alumni game that would be taking place about an hour after our arrival.

Gradually, players from the Amerks as well as alumni started to arrive at the arena. With pucks in hand, we approached the players we recognized to ask for an autograph. At that level, the players are still more than happy to oblige their fans. Some of them even thanked us for asking them! We talked to a few players and alumni and got a few autographs. But in our haste to chase down NHL prospects like Clarke MacArthur, we almost let one of the biggest prizes slip right through our fingers!

Don and I had read on the Amerks site that Charron is the nephew of Jim

Craig, the goalie who led the underdog United States Olympic Hockey Team to a gold medal in the 1980 Winter Olympics. You know, the "Miracle On Ice" and "Do You Believe In Miracles" team.

Yes, that team.

We had no idea that Jim Craig, the goaltender who wrapped himself in the American flag after his team's shocking upset of the extremely talented Russian squad, would be in Rochester that day. Sure enough, a car pulls up to the players' entrance and a well-dressed, middle-aged gentleman exits and heads to the arena door. We had no idea it was Jim Craig. He walked right past us and through the doors, and as they were closing, we heard someone inside say, "Hi, Uncle Jim!"

It took about 10 second for that to sink in, and then Don and I looked at each other, both with a stunned look on our face, and at the exact same time uttered the exact same words: "Uncle Jim?"

We had missed a living legend.

Fortunately, the alumni game was about to begin so we walked to the arena's main entrance to see if we could get in. Much to our surprise, the doors were unlocked and there was no security in sight. Once inside, there were maybe a few dozen other spectators, mostly family members and friends of the players and alumni. We walked right down to the players' entrance to the bench, our pockets stuffed with hockey pucks and a silver Sharpie in hand. A few minutes later, Jim Craig was heading toward the players' bench to watch the game, standing just a few feet from me, Don and Kenny.

The hockey folk hero turned out to be a great guy. He signed Kenny's Sabres cap, and then proceeded to sign a couple of pucks for both me and Don. We also had a brief but rather nice conversation with him. As soon as I returned to my seat, I got out my cell phone and called Maureen. I was so excited ... like a little kid meeting his hero.

At the end of the day Don and I had a couple dozen autographed hockey pucks and got to watch both the alumni game and the Amerks game later that night. And best of all, we'll always have a great story to tell about meeting — but almost missing — one of the greatest American hockey heroes of all time!

My other favorite autograph story centers around my son Andrew, who has always enjoyed watching wrestling on television, and has had a few opportunities to attend WWE (World Wrestling Entertainment) events at HSBC Arena in Buffalo.

When he was 17, the WWE had an event planned in Buffalo and Andrew had tickets to the event. Not just ordinary tickets, but tickets in a luxury suite courtesy of Maureen's boss. Unfortunately, he would later find out that he had to work that night. To make things worse, he absolutely hated his job, working at a fast-food chain that specializes in subs. He hated working with food and having to clean up after other people. Let's just say he wasn't cut out for the fast-food industry and leave it at that.

Andrew would have to give up his tickets and miss the WWE event, which was to include a big match featuring Shawn Michaels, aka "The Heartbreak Kid." He wasn't very happy about that but I will give him credit ... he did go to work that night.

Late in the evening, just before closing, the doors to the restaurant swing open and who walks in? None other than Shawn Michaels, of course. The wrestler had completed his match and was heading down the New York State Thruway when he must have had a craving for a tuna salad with extra tuna. For some strange twist of fate, he would choose to exit onto a road that would lead him directly to Andrew.

Andrew never thought to ask the hulking wrestler for an autograph but was able to engage in some small talk with him. For the next several weeks, he shared the story dozens of times with anyone who would listen.

It was one memorable night in an otherwise totally forgettable fast-food career.

Chapter 13
The Cuban Sandwich

The following story is not a *Seinfeld* episode, although the wacky twists and turns that it takes would make Jerry, George, Kramer and Elaine proud.

Surely you've heard the expression "everything happens for a reason." Well, here's proof.

The story begins in the Florida home of my cousin Jimmy and his lovely wife Marie. My brothers, mother and I are in Florida for my nephew's beach wedding, and we have a few hours to kill on Sunday before our return flight to Buffalo. For some reason, the conversation turns to talk of Cuban sandwiches. I had never had one, nor had I ever even heard of the Cuban sandwich.

Marie, who was born in Cuba, tells us how delicious they are. But that's it. The sandwich conversation doesn't go much further.

I returned home from Florida Sunday night, knowing that in one week I would be traveling to Boston with Maureen and the kids for Lauren's dance competition. I don't get to Boston often, and I very much wanted to take in a baseball game at Fenway Park. I had been to Fenway once before and actually saw a double-header back in the day when teams actually played double-headers. Three things I remember about that day was that it was freezing out, that Wade Boggs went something like 0 for 9 at the plate, and that Nolan Ryan was in town with the visitors but was scratched due to the cold weather.

For a couple of weeks I kept looking online to see if I could buy Red Sox tickets, but all the sellers were looking for scalper prices. A few days before we left for Boston, I put an ad on Craigslist saying that I was looking for four tickets to the Monday night game. I continued to answer ads, but everyone was either asking for too much money or had already sold their tickets.

In my ad I mentioned that I would be willing to pay cash or possibly trade some of my extra autographed sports memorabilia for tickets. No bites. We headed to Boston, ticketless.

Sunday evening I was checking Craigslist and came across a guy selling four standing room only seats for $35 each. I responded to the ad and he still had the tickets. Then I tried to talk him down a bit on the price, to which he responded that other people were also interested. He'd let me know Monday afternoon. That was cutting it a little close.

Monday morning I checked my e-mail and there was a response to my ad seeking tickets to that day's game. The guy said he had four tickets and was only looking for face value, $45 each. So I asked where the tickets were located. Right behind home plate, was his response.

"I'll take them!" I said, without a moment's hesitation.

We talked on the phone a couple of times and "Tom" agreed to meet me at the hotel to drop off the tickets. He pulled up to the hotel, with his wife, in a black Lexus.

"These are my season tickets," Tom said, "and I've never sold them before. We never miss a game, but we just got back into town and couldn't make the game. A friend was going to use the tickets, but he backed out at the last minute." So Tom sold me his four tickets for a total of $180.

Before they pulled away, his wife mentioned that the seats are one section away from where the players' wives, girlfriends and families sit. And then Tom, probably recalling the mention of memorabilia in my Craigslist ad, told me that former Red Sox pitcher Luis Tiant has a food stand outside of Fenway, and that he's usually there signing autographs on game days.

After closing the deal with Tom, I headed to the mall attached to our hotel and was able to find one leather-covered baseball. There were plenty of baseballs with synthetic covers, but those aren't good for autographs. But for some reason, the store had one lone leather baseball still sitting on the shelf. I bought it and took it to Fenway just in case Tiant would be there.

Early that evening, Andrew and I, along with two other boys around Andrew's age — brothers of Lauren's dancing friends — hiked over to Fenway Park. Before entering, we walked around the exterior of the stadium in search of Tiant's food stand. Andrew was the first to spot it. Sure enough, the Cuban-born pitcher was sitting there signing autographs for customers, just like Tom had said.

And what was he selling at his stand? Cuban sandwiches, of course!

Marie was right, they are delicious.

Tom's tickets were outstanding. Directly behind home plate, just as he had promised.

We walked around the entire stadium, inside and out. We watched batting practice from atop the Green Monster. We watched as a rookie pitcher from Oakland tossed a rare complete game two-hitter. We joined the Fenway faithful in a long standing ovation for Nomar Garciaparra, who was making his first return to Fenway that evening.

We enjoyed the day. Thoroughly.

Chapter 14
Wrestling With Career Choices

I wrote an article for *The Buffalo News* not too long ago that focused on how, in some families, the sport of wrestling is literally handed down from generation to generation. Take, for example, two of the men that I interviewed for that piece, Ted DiBiase Jr. and Cody Rhodes, both stars in the WWE as of this writing.

DiBiase Jr. is the son of Ted "The Million Dollar Man" DiBiase and the step-grandson of "Iron" Mike DiBiase. Even his grandmother — yes, you read that right, his grandmother — Helen Hild, was a professional wrestler.

Same type of situation for Rhodes, who also grew up in a wrestling environment. Cody is the son of Dusty

Rhodes and the step-brother of Dustin "Goldust" Rhodes. Two of his uncles, Jerry Sags and Fred Ottman, better known to wrestling fans as "Typhoon" and "Tugboat," also found fame within the ring, as did Cody's godfather, Terry "Magnum T.A." Allen.

"It was my childhood dream to be a wrestler," DiBiase told me. "I wanted to be a wrestler just like my dad. When I was in high school, it was pretty incredible to come home from school with my buddies, turn on the TV and see my dad. He wasn't an accountant or a dentist like the other dads. He was a wrestler. It was cool. It was different."

At first, DiBiase's father wasn't thrilled with his son's decision to follow in his footsteps. "My father wanted me as far away from the business as possible," admitted DiBiase. "There's a bit of the rock star lifestyle, and that can be hard on a family. My father was probably away from home for 75 percent of my childhood. That takes a toll on a family. But my dad was always an incredible father. He did a great job as dad when he was home, and always stayed in touch when he was on the road."

Rhodes echoed a similar experience growing up as the son of a famous wrestler.

"I always saw my dad in a heroic light," he said. "To the fans, my dad was also a hero. You see that, and you can't help but want to be part of it. Originally, my dad didn't want me to get into wrestling, but now I think he's happy that I'm carrying on the family legacy. My goal is to become the World Heavyweight Champion and hold the same title that my father had."

What can you say? Fathers, sons and sports. It's a special bond.

Back in the 1950s, Ilio DiPaolo was making a name for himself in the wrestling ring. He won countless matches with his "airplane spin" finishing move, hoisting the other wrestler onto his massive shoulders and spinning him around in the center of the ring, before dropping him to the canvas and covering him for a count of three.

But it wasn't the glamour life that today's professional athletes enjoy. Ilio and his family would travel from one city to the next in their Cadillac, which also served as their living quarters from time to time. And if for some reason you were unable to make it to the next venue, you didn't get paid. It was that simple.

And then there's the physical toll of wrestling.

"My father suffered from separated shoulders and broken ribs from being thrown out of the ring, a hernia from lifting a 350-pound wrestler over his head, concussions from being thrown onto the floor, neck and back injuries from being body slammed, and underwent eight ankle operations," said Ilio's oldest son, Dennis, a good friend of mine. "The body can't take that punishment six or seven days a week."

"It was a difficult lifestyle," added Dennis, who, as a youngster, often traveled with his parents from city to city. "My father didn't really want his family to be constantly on the road. He eventually settled in Buffalo because of the fan base — the people. The people here made him feel more at home than any other city. He felt an attraction to the community."

Ilio would go on to open a restaurant in Blasdell, N.Y., just outside of Buffalo, called Ilio DiPaolo's Restaurant and

Ringside Lounge. Rather than follow their father into the ring, sons Dennis and Michael joined him in the restaurant business. Michael graduated from the Culinary Institute of America and serves as the restaurant's executive chef, while Dennis oversees the business end. "We make a great tag team," said Michael, pun definitely intended.

Tragically, Ilio was struck by a car and killed in 1995. His legend, however, lives on. His restaurant remains a popular destination, frequently visited by professional athletes and especially by members of the Buffalo Bills. Ilio's wrestling memorabilia is featured prominently throughout the restaurant. Scholarships are given annually in his name.

If Ilio were alive today, he'd be the first to tell you he was grateful that his sons followed him into the restaurant business rather than into the ring. Of Dennis and Michael, it was Michael who came closest to a wrestling career. He was a member of the varsity wrestling squad at Ashland College during his freshman year before having a change of heart and transferring to the Culinary Institute.

Dennis, on the other hand, wanted no part of the ring, although he was almost thrown into a professional match as a child of just seven or eight years of age. You see, Dennis had traveled with his dad to a wrestling venue, where they were approached by a worried promoter. The announced card that night featured several matches, including a midget tag team match. But there was a problem — only three of the four midgets showed up.

Dennis was the right size. The promoter asked Ilio if Dennis could "just go stand in the corner" during the match. He wouldn't have to be involved, the promoter promised. Young but smart, Dennis wasn't buying any of it. He begged his father not to make him go into the ring.

And with that, Ilio finally turned to the promoter and said, in broken English, "What can I do? The boy doesn't want to wrestle."

I'm sure the promoter wasn't pleased, but seriously ... what was he going to do about it? I had the pleasure of meeting

Ilio a couple of times at his restaurant and the man was a giant. His hands were easily twice the size of mine.

No one in their right mind would ever mess with him.

Chapter 15
Goin' to the Dogs

Is there anything cuter than a boy playing with a puppy? The dog lapping away at the little guy's face, the smell of puppy chow on his breath ... the dog, not the boy.

I've always had a dog at my side, from boyhood straight through adulthood. Our first real pet — not counting goldfish and turtles — was Peanuts, a beagle mix. The most memorable thing about Peanuts was that he was scared of his own shadow. Thunder and other loud noises would drive him into a complete frenzy. He also liked to jump, like the time he jumped over the chain link fence in our yard. The only problem was that his leash was attached to the bottom of the fence, and Peanuts didn't quite make it to the ground on the other side. Nope, came about three feet short of the ground to be exact. Had our neighbor not been looking out his window at that exact moment, Peanuts would have died of an apparent suicide.

No fence could contain that dog, and Peanuts finally made one escape too many. We were notified that his remains were picked up on a busy street about a mile from our home. I was devastated.

It didn't take long to convince my mom and dad that we needed another dog. Enter Smokey, a Cocker Spaniel and Manchester Terrier mix so named because his coat was almost completely black. Unlike Peanuts, Smokey was very memorable. He was quite possibly the best and most athletic dog ever to roam our planet.

Smokey made an immediate impression on me, my father and my brother Mark. While my mother was drawn to one of Smokey's siblings that was, admittedly, very cute and cuddly, Smokey's antics quickly drew our attention. He was a bundle of energy — small but extremely fast and incredibly goofy. He chased everything around the seller's house, including the other dogs, a cat, and people. There was no question that he was the one that would be going home with us. It was the best $30 we ever spent.

Smokey turned out to be a terrific companion, always ready for a walk, or, better yet, a game of catch. He was a marvelous athlete. For example, I would throw a Frisbee the length of two houses, and Smokey would run it down and catch it in flight. I could also take a tennis ball and throw it as high into the sky as possible, and Smokey would get right under it and catch it. He rarely missed, and he never was the first to quit. His game always outlasted mine.

The Smokester was also fascinated by a simple stream of water shot from a garden hose. Send a steady stream across the yard, and Smokey would jump up and try to catch it in his mouth. He also enjoyed playing with balloons. Toss one into the air and he'd punch it right back to you with his nose. He'd play for hours and hours if he could.

Smokey lived to be 16. Our entire family was heartbroken when he had to be put down, finally becoming too old and too frail to walk from one room to the next. He was much more than a dog to me ... more like a fourth brother.

Maureen also had several dogs while growing up in Buffalo, so shortly after we purchased our first house we also found our first dog together. Allie, a Fox Terrier and Poodle mix, was a tiny little thing, about 10 pounds dripping wet. We got her for free from a family who's dog had puppies. "Free" lasted just a couple of hours.

When I brought Allie home, I noticed that she seemed to be scratching herself a lot. Upon close examination, I quickly discovered the reason why. Fleas. She was covered with them. I made a mad dash to the closest store where I purchased an assortment of shampoos, flea collars and various other bug-killing agents. Upon returning home, I immediately dipped Allie into a flea bath, which apparently infuriated the fleas. Instead of dying a quick death like they were supposed to — that's what the label on the bottle said — they immediately took shelter in Allie's ears, making her howl in pain. Next stop: doggie emergency room.

A couple of hundred dollars later and Allie was good as new and fresh as a daisy. The staff at the emergency room had to pick the fleas off her one by one. They did a great job, I have to admit.

As dogs go, Allie was no Smokey. She wasn't a big fan of people, and she liked to bark a lot. And she never really got a good handle on the whole house-breaking thing.

Allie passed away at the relatively young age of nine. But before she died, she did one thing for which I'll be eternally grateful. She saved our house from perhaps burning to the ground, with us in it.

It was a Saturday night, I believe, and we had been away for most of the day. When we returned home, I let Allie out into our attached garage so she could then run into the back yard through a doggie door. But something was odd. Allie stayed in the garage and kept barking. Even when I opened the door and yelled at her to get in the house, she just stood in the center of the garage, staring off into a corner and barking relentlessly. I was about two steps into the garage when I spotted flames shooting out from beneath the wood paneling that lined the garage wall. As fate would have it, I had a fire extinguisher just a few feet away. As I emptied the canister, Maureen called the fire department. They arrived within minutes.

Upon investigation, a fireman found the problem. A mouse had built a nest behind the paneling and then decided to chomp down on some tasty wiring. Sparks from the wire set the nest on fire (and the mouse as well). One of the firemen had me identify the charred remains.

If it had happened earlier in the day while we were gone, or later in the evening when we were asleep, I'm convinced that our house would have burned to the ground. Had Allie not spotted the sparks and flames and barked and barked until she had our attention, our house might have suffered severe damage. That fire would have crept right up the wall. Above that wall and ceiling? Andrew and Lauren's bedrooms. I don't like to think about it.

The next day, Allie received some very special treats.

When Allie died, Andrew was heartbroken. All he wanted for his approaching birthday and Christmas was a new dog. How could we say no?

Enter Rudy (short for Rudolph). To this day, Maureen kids me that I could have easily written the equivalent of *Marley & Me*. A Golden Retriever, Rudy is best described as a big goof with an endless appetite. Oh, how he loved to eat, and not just his own food. If you turned your head for even a second, your slice of pizza or hot dog vanished into thin air. About the only time he ever slowed down was after one of his storied eating binges.

It was just after Christmas 2008 and we had all gone to the movies. The Christmas gifts were still under the tree, including a plastic one-pound container of Muscle Milk, a protein mix that Andrew had requested. Well, it seems that we forgot to block off the living room and Rudy found the vanilla-flavored Muscle Milk. He ate the cardboard box, devoured much of the plastic container, and then feasted on the delicious pound of powder inside. The evidence covered his entire face.

Bloated and full for the first time in his life, Rudy just curled up on the family room rug for about the next 12 hours with a content look upon his face.

Rudy could never jump a fence or catch a ball. In fact, if you threw a ball at him, it usually just bounced off his gigantic forehead. And he certainly never saved our house from burning down. But, oh, how I loved that big, goofy, smelly dog.

At the age of 12 and in failing health, Rudy became very sick as I was finishing this chapter. He stopped eating on a Tuesday. By Friday, he was too weak to stand. Andrew and I had the incredibly heartbreaking task of taking him to the vet to be put down. We both broke down and cried. We miss him terribly.

Is there another dog somewhere down the line that will replace him?

I doubt it. He's irreplaceable.

Chapter 16
Dancing Around the Truth

Is dance an art or a sport? Are dancers artists or athletes? I've been wondering about that for years. I really have. Seriously.

Dancing is in the Olympics, so is that alone enough to qualify it as a sport? My daughter Lauren has been dancing since the age of 3 — she's in her late teens now. We've traveled with her to various competitions over the years, and I remember one older female judge getting on stage and emphatically telling the participants that they are indeed artists, not athletes. Yet, in addition to taking structured classes several days a week nearly year-round, Lauren and her fellow dancers also have to run laps and do sit-ups, push-ups, stomach crunches and various other exercises almost daily. There are days when she comes home with more bruises than Mike

Tyson's sparring partner. I'd like to see my "athlete" friends keep up with her fitness routine.

I'm also amazed by the fact that she can do complete flips in midair. Once, during an acrobatic routine — ironically being performed to the song *Kung Fu Fighting* — Lauren did a flip in the air and accidentally kicked her friend Emily right in the face! Emily, to her credit, finished the dance. Within minutes, one side of Emily's face was completely swollen and discolored. It was one of the worst facial bruises I had ever seen, proving that dancers are pretty tough customers indeed.

I don't see a lot of artists getting kicked in the face.

On the other hand, the choreographed movements and motion on stage are often enough to bring audiences to tears. Rarely do you see tears at a sporting event, unless maybe your hometown team just won a Super Bowl or Stanley Cup. Sadly, we've never experienced those tears of joys in Buffalo.

While I've always considered myself to be fairly athletic, I've never been a dancer. Sure, you may catch me doing the occasional slow dance with my wife at a wedding, but that doesn't really count as dancing, does it? Anyone can do that.

I've never been one to fast dance, and I think I know why. First, I went to an all-boys Catholic high school. Sure, they had dances and I would attend with my buddies, but it was always the same routine: band on stage, girls on the dance floor, and boys standing along the walls watching the girls and trying to act cool. Any guy who actually made it onto the dance floor was either lucky enough to be slow-dancing with a beautiful young lady or had a death wish. At a school where you had to be an athlete to be considered cool, dancing was definitely not viewed as a sport.

And then there were the company dances that Maureen's former employer seemed to host at least a couple of times every year, usually around Valentine's Day and the Christmas holidays. We'd be sitting around the table with her friends having a nice discussion and enjoying the food and drinks when, sure enough, some poor sap of a guy would get dragged onto the dance floor by his date. The women seated at our table would then share a secret laugh about the poor guy's dancing skills ... or should I say lack of dancing skills. I'm sure the guy didn't want to be up there in the first place, and now he's got countless sets of eyes watching his every move.

Just when I'm feeling sorry for the poor guy, the women seated at my table would decide it's time to dance, and suddenly I'm dragged onto the dance floor against my will, even though that's the last place on Earth I want to be and because I know they'll soon be sharing a private laugh about my obvious lack of dancing skills.

Yes, I know. There's a comfortable leather couch in some psychiatrist's office with my name on it.

But back to Lauren and the real dancers ... athletes or artists?

I think my mind was finally made up on a trip to Boston for one of Lauren's national dance competitions. By the end of five long days of classes and competing, I saw countless participants limping around with the aid of knee braces, ankle wraps and crutches, not to mention ice packs applied to just about every body part that can be pulled, twisted or simply overused.

I imagine you'd see the same type of thing in the training room of a professional football team after two-a-day practices or a hockey team after an encounter with a very physical opponent.

You just don't see that physical toll in the art world. So for what it's worth, I'm going to say that dance is an art but dancers are indeed athletes.

One final thought on the subject: What is it that we tell a dancer before he or she goes on stage? "Break a leg."

And sometimes, they do!

Chapter 17
Most Likely to Survive

Matt Faulkner never gave a lot of thought to sports. In fact, the only reason I know Matt and his family is because his parents — Skip and Pam — signed him up for T-ball the same year that my daughter Lauren wanted to play. It was the only year that Matt took part in an organized sports league.

Even though he was just 5 or 6 years old at the time and more than a dozen years have passed since then, Matt was one of those kids I could never forget. He was small for his age but had a constant smile on his face, and that smile stretched from ear to ear. You'd see him walking toward the baseball diamond in his bulky team shirt and a hat that looked way too big for his head, and you couldn't help but smile yourself.

Matt and Lauren would attend the same elementary, middle and high

school, so I'd hear his name or see him
from time to time. I have no idea if he
remembered me as his one and only
coach or the fact that he even played T-
ball. And while he didn't participate on
any of the school sports teams, he was
involved in several other activities and
was an excellent student.

During his senior year of high school,
his classmates voted him "Most Likely to
Succeed" and "Most Involved." The self-
proclaimed president of the National
Honor Society and editor of the high
school yearbook, he earned a
scholarship to attend Canisius College
in Buffalo, where he wanted to study
finance and earn his MBA before
landing a job as a financial analyst.

Unlike a lot of other kids his age, Matt
had his future planned out.

Life would have a different plan. That
plan went into effect on March 2, 2009.

Matt doesn't remember much of what
happened that day. He now knows what
happened, only because his friends and
family have pieced the story together for
him.

He recalls very little of his after-
school trip to the nearby Village of East

Aurora with three friends, or the fact that they stopped at Vidler's 5 & 10 and then a small cafe to have some dinner. As they prepared to head home to West Seneca, Matt would settle into the back seat, directly behind the driver.

They didn't get very far.

Shortly after exiting the Thruway, their car was t-boned by another vehicle. The door next to Matt took the full impact. His friends escaped serious injury, but Matt would not be so lucky. His return home would be delayed by 103 days.

Unconscious, Matt was flown by Mercy Flight to the Trauma Center at the Erie County Medical Center (ECMC), where he would remain in a coma for two months.

"It's not like you see on TV ... you don't just wake up from a coma one day," Matt told me as we met for lunch in October of 2009, some seven months after the accident. "You wake up slowly. At first, you're only conscious for a few minutes or maybe an hour a day. I don't recall a full day (of consciousness) until May 5th."

Although he was now conscious, he didn't and couldn't understand what was wrong with him. His mind was telling him that he was fine, and that everyone was "betraying" him — including his parents — and he didn't know why.

Two months in a coma can be devastating to the human body. Matt suffered from abnormal limb "posturing" due to atrophy. In simple terms, his hands, feet, arms and legs were showing the not-so-pleasant effects of lack of use.

Still unaware of his serious medical condition, Matt tried to escape from his hospital bed. He hit the ground hard.

"It was my moment of realization," he said.

The fact that Matt even came out of the coma was a miracle. During his first week at the hospital, one of his many doctors told his parents they might have to make a decision that no parent ever wants to make — the decision of whether or not to keep their severely injured son on life support.

As he slowly came out of the coma, Matt found himself unable to speak. He could move his mouth, but was unable to talk, suffering from something called "dysarthria." On May 9th, his voice began to come back as a whisper.

"The next day, my voice just cracked and then it was there," Matt said. That was Mother's Day. Matt spoke his first words since the accident that came out above a whisper.

"I said, 'Happy Mother's Day, Mom.' She cried. Needless to say, she was elated," Matt recalled.

Intensive, painful therapy would fill Matt's days for the next several weeks. He started to walk again in June, having to use a walker for assistance for just a week. He also attended occupational and speech therapy sessions every weekday, and in typical Matt Faulkner style, made friends with many of the therapists on the hospital's staff.

Finally, on June 12, 2009, Matt was released from the hospital. He would finally return home, 103 days after an afternoon trip with friends to a quaint village just a few short miles from his hometown.

"Getting out of the hospital was the best day of my life," Matt said. A Hummer limo, compliments of his grandmother, waited outside to pick him up. It was packed with family and friends — including his parents and sisters, Rachel and Nicole — who would accompany Matt on the joyful and thankfully uneventful ride home. When they finally reached their destination, Matt found his front yard loaded with well-wishers celebrating his arrival.

Matt was most proud of the fact that he was able to walk out of ECMC, to the awaiting limo, without the aid of a wheelchair. "My attending physician told my mom that they would get me to walk out of here." He was right.

Twelve days after he was released, Matt walked across the stage at his high school graduation ceremony. Cheers — and tears — filled the auditorium.

Today, Matt's doctors are predicting a full recovery, but it certainly won't be easy. He must still go through his physical therapy exercises at home to help build his strength, and appointments with occupational, speech and vision therapists still fill his calendar.

Slowly but surely, life is returning to normal. Matt is once again teaching religious education to fourth grade students at St. John Vianney parish. And while Canisius College held his scholarship for a year, he enrolled in two classes at Erie Community College, including a public speaking course. During his first presentation to the class, he discussed his brain injury. He later returned to his part-time job at the local mall, and eventually achieved his goal of attending Canisius College.

"I still have the same goals as before," Matt said, that once familiar smile starting to stretch across his face again. "Nothing is going to stop me. I'm very determined."

Chapter 18
Going to Bat for Organ Donation

Fortunate. Blessed. Lucky. Humbled. Those are words that Jonathan Dandes, president of Rich Baseball Operations, uses to describe his life today. And it has nothing to do with the fact that he has what many of us would consider a dream job with the Buffalo Bisons and a great office overlooking the baseball diamond within beautiful Coca-Cola Field in downtown Buffalo.

If you really had to think about it, what words would you use if you were given a second chance at life courtesy of the talented transplant team at the Erie County Medical Center? And what if the healthy kidney that you received was unselfishly donated by a good friend who wanted absolutely nothing in return?

All of which brings us back to fortunate, blessed, lucky and humbled.

Jon was diagnosed with kidney disease 14 years ago through routine testing. "I was fortunate," he said. "I had gone for a routine physical, and the blood test came back a little funny. As a result, I had to go for further testing, and the diagnosis was kidney disease.

"I was fortunate that my nephrologist was able to keep my kidney disease at bay for 12 years through a series of medications. My condition was monitored very carefully, but then my creatinine level spiked. In a period of about three months it went to a level where I had to go for dialysis two times a week." He chose to receive his treatments at ECMC.

"First, I want to say that dialysis nurses are special people," said Jon. "As a patient, it was sort of an out-of-body experience for me, watching the blood flow out of my body and into a machine that cleaned it and then pumped it back into my body. I spent a lot of hours there, and I spent a lot of that time talking to God."

Knowing he would soon need a kidney transplant, Jon's wife, Marcy, offered one of hers. At first thought to be a good match, it wasn't until the very last test was conducted that doctors would determine that Marcy's kidney would not be suitable for Jon.

Eventually, news of a compatible donor would come. This kidney, much to Jon's surprise, would come from a good friend who had gone through the testing process without Jon's knowledge. The call came from Jon's transplant coordinator at ECMC, Marcia Kryzwicki.

"I received my new kidney from a good friend who has chosen to remain anonymous ... and now we're even closer. It was very special. What can I say about the guy? He saved my life. The only request he had was for a room at the other end of the hall from me. He knew my room was going to be crazy, and he didn't want to go through that," Jon said with a laugh.

Heading into the surgery, Jon admits to spending a lot of time talking to God and making promises.

"I couldn't have gone through this without the support of my family and some very close friends, including the people I work for. Bob and Mindy Rich were spectacular, as were my colleagues and associates at Rich Baseball. My wife, Marcy ... I wouldn't be sitting here today if it wasn't for all of her support — the nursing care, putting up with my mood swings, and her assurances that everything would be OK. If there's an MVP in all of this, it's Marcy. She was — and still is — spectacular. I'm very fortunate.

"I also had an absolutely extraordinary medical team led by Dr. Rocco Venuto and Dr. George Blessios. I had been to the Cleveland Clinic and they told me to see Dr. Venuto and said that I'd be in great shape."

They were right. The transplant would take place on February 16, 2007. Jon remembers the date like he would his own birthday.

"I really don't remember much about the surgery other than the great anticipation leading up to it and the big group of my family and friends at the hospital," Jon said. "After I woke up, I remember seeing smiles all around and being told that the surgery went great.

My immediate concern was for my donor. A day later he walked into my room. I thought, how do I repay something like that?"

The answer: volunteerism. Since his successful surgery, Jon jokes that he has become the "poster child" for transplants.

"Maybe I can repay everyone by helping others who are going through this, so that's what I try to do," said Jon, who has served as vice chairman of Upstate New York Transplant Services (UNYTS), and on the board of directors of the National Kidney Foundation of Western New York. "My goal now is to take my experience and help people to understand that they can make a difference as organ donors, and that 'donate life' is not just a slogan. I also want to tell people that early detection is critical. We need to educate the public."

In addition to volunteering on behalf of those organizations, Jon's life has changed in other ways since his transplant. The bad changes — taking 25 to 50 anti-rejection pills and other pills daily to combat side effects, for example — are far outnumbered by the positive changes.

The things he once took for granted, he hopes he doesn't anymore. There's a renewed sense of family and with it a greater appreciation for his wife, his son, his daughter. He also has a greater sense of appreciation and thankfulness for the colleagues and friends who helped him through his medical crisis.

Working in a sports environment gives Jon an opportunity to share his message with crowds of people, and he's done so by bringing some kidney and donor-related awareness and fundraising events to Coca-Cola Field. He'd like to show people that the real heroes in Western New York aren't necessarily found on baseball diamonds, football fields or ice rinks.

The real heroes in life, according to Jon, are found at home, in doctors' offices and hospitals, and working alongside of you day after day.

It's having those people in our lives that make us feel fortunate. Blessed. Lucky. Humbled.

Chapter 19
A Lifetime of Giving

My friend Hugo Kahn has witnessed humanity at its worst. Born in 1915 in Horhausen, Germany, his parents and a younger sister were among the 11 million victims of the Holocaust.

Now 95, Hugo cherishes every moment of his life and never stops giving back to the community. Those in Western New York fortunate enough to know Hugo — and the countless families who have benefitted from his kindness — are living witnesses to humanity at its best.

It was 1936 when Hugo arrived in the United States aboard the S.S. Washington. "When we were 15 miles away from Germany, an announcement was made telling us that we were now free," Hugo recalled. "You should have heard the screaming and hollering." That joy has stayed with Hugo for the past 70-plus years.

Hugo would go on to serve four years in the United States Army, doing whatever he could to help his new country defeat Adolf Hitler and the Nazi party. He would meet and marry Ann, the love of his life, and together they would raise a beautiful daughter, Eva, who would grow up to be a teacher and librarian. Hugo and Ann have now been married for 68 years, and while their health may be failing, their love has never faltered.

In Germany, life was a daily struggle for the Kahn family. In the United States, Hugo Kahn is happy to share whatever he has with those who are struggling.

"I've changed my attitude from being an angry soldier who did his best against the Nazi machine to a guy who just wants to live another day. I had to forgive a long time ago ... but I will never forget."

In 1983, after his retirement from the Sattler's Department Store, Hugo began a relationship with the Food Bank of Western New York that continues to this day. Inside the Food Bank's offices at

91 Holt Street in Buffalo sits a modest cubicle featuring photos of Hugo Kahn's family along with several items promoting his favorite sports team, the Buffalo Bills. His official title is "public relations advisor."

"I was looking for something worthwhile to do," said Hugo in response to how his relationship with the nonprofit organization began. "Someone told me they were looking for people to help out at the Food Bank. I told them that I didn't know anything about food except for what was on the plate in front of me! They just told me to 'make friends and things will happen.' They were right. I've learned to be a goodwill ambassador."

Part of that goodwill relates back to his love for the Buffalo Bills. Hugo has been a member of the Monday Quarterback Club — a group of local business people who support the team — for as long as anyone can remember. He faithfully attends all of the Club's luncheons throughout the football season, and he never goes alone. At each luncheon he's surrounded by a table full of Food Bank supporters, usually people from the local food industry and members of the media who can help spread the Food Bank's message. Hugo pays for each of his guests out of his own pocket.

"I pay for these lunches out of my own pocket because I want people to know that every donation they make to the Food Bank is used to feed the hungry," Hugo said.

His acts of kindness have not gone unnoticed. Thanks to his efforts on behalf of the Food Bank, he has become close friends with Bills owner Ralph Wilson and his wife Mary. In fact, Hugo received a personal invitation from the Wilsons to be their guest at Ralph's Hall of Fame induction in Canton, Ohio, in August 2009.

"Through the Monday Quarterback Club, I've met some terrific people," said Hugo. "I've gone from growing up in a small town in Germany to knowing the owner of the Buffalo Bills. The Wilsons are great people who have done a terrific job with the Bills, the Monday Quarterback Club and the Food Bank."

While he was unable to join the Wilsons in Canton, Hugo was not far from their thoughts. Just a few days after the Hall of Fame induction, Hugo received a package in the mail. It was from Ralph and Mary Wilson and it contained several mementos from induction weekend, including a hat featuring an embroidered Ralph Wilson signature. Hugo was overwhelmed by their act of friendship. "I can't think of a nicer couple," he added.

Every year, with assistance from people like Hugo Kahn, the Food Bank of WNY distributes 12 million pounds of food throughout the community, serving more than 100,000 people each month. The need is year-round and growing. It's why Hugo keeps on giving, even at the age of 95.

"Whatever happened yesterday, forget about it. Do whatever you can today."

Words to live by courtesy of Hugo Kahn, a man who does whatever he can ... every single day.

Chapter 20
Life is More Than Just a Game

So here I am approaching age 50, still playing softball twice a week. Gary remains my catcher, although he missed most of the 2009 season due to knee surgery. Squatting behind home plate for well over 20 years will take its toll on the knees, I would imagine.

Once completely surrounded on the field by guys approximately my age, that has changed in recent years. Remember all those boys I coached through years of house baseball? The kids who came together as a team at that one memorable Saturday morning practice? The team that would go on to win a championship together after years of losing seasons?

Well, several of them, including Andrew, have now joined me on the softball diamond. Come to one of our games and you'll also find the quick-footed Matt and Joey patrolling the outfield. Nothing like young legs to chase down those fly balls.

In the infield you'll find Tom playing first base, and Matt's younger brother Corey entrenched at second base. Mitch, the skilled right-hander who played against us in the baseball championship game, would join our baseball team the following year and later played several infield positions on our softball team. Brandon, the inexperienced pitcher who earned the victory in our championship game, joined the softball team late in the 2009 season as an injury replacement. As my older teammates retire, I hope to continue to add players from that very special baseball team.

It's hard to explain, but there was a special bond between me and those boys. While most came from very good families, I still felt like a father to many of them, and in many ways that bond still exists. I have to imagine that the boys feel the same way. Why else would they want to come back and play softball with me after all these years?

While I'll probably never know their reasons for joining me on the softball diamond, I think it may have something to do with the fact that I always tried to teach them more than just baseball skills. I tried to teach them about life and how to be good people. I taught them about respect — respect for their teammates, opponents, coaches, parents and umpires. While other teams would regularly trash talk their opponents and argue with umpires, I never allowed those things on my team. Win or lose, we conducted ourselves as gentlemen. Even after a bitter loss, we'd suck it up, shake hands with our opponents and congratulate them on having played a great game.

I have a feeling that my relationship with these young men will continue for many years to come. Now in their early twenties, it won't be long before they graduate from college, begin their careers and start having families of their own. I hope to be there as they graduate and get married, and it would be especially rewarding to someday see them on the ball diamonds of Western New York, teaching their children and others how to throw to the cutoff man or lay down a successful bunt without getting their fingers crushed by the ball in the process.

Until that day, we'll continue to get together on Wednesday evenings throughout the spring and summer months and just play some ball. I will cherish each and every game no matter how many — or how few — I have left in me.

-End

About the Author

Joe Kirchmyer grew up in a neighborhood where families cleared the fields behind their modest homes to create their own hidden baseball diamond, football field and hockey pond. It was a neighborhood of old orchards, fishing ponds, mature trees and railroad tracks. To him, it was heaven on earth.

Joe discovered his love of writing at a very young age and went on to major in journalism at Buffalo State College. Following a 25-year career as a reporter, editor and marketing professional, he opened his own communications company called Kirchmyer Media. He currently resides in West Seneca, N.Y., a suburb of Buffalo, and is still chasing his dreams. You can contact him at jkirchmyer@verizon.net.

www.ingramcontent.com/pod-product-compliance
Lightning Source LLC
Chambersburg PA
CBHW060303050426
42448CB00009B/1731